TRAINING COLLEGE STUDENTS IN INFORMATION LITERACY

Profiles of How Colleges Teach Their Students to Use Academic Libraries

TABLE OF CONTENTS

PRIMARY RESEARCH GROUP INC.   WWW.PRIMARYRESEARCH.COM

INTRODUCTION

The ability to use a library is such a fundamental skill in higher education that a small investment in library education can make a big difference in the academic careers of many students. As the array of resources offered by libraries, and over the internet, has grown enormously in the past ten years, the need for library training in academic libraries has grown commensurately. However, the resources, facilities and support granted to libraries to accomplish their educational ends have often not grown in step with the new educational responsibilities.

This report is an attempt to profile how nine North American academic libraries are dealing with this new dilemma. Although the sample is somewhat top heavy with major research and doctoral level institutions, we have also chosen some smaller colleges to get a sense of how they are dealing with the emerging flood of library education demands.

Although each library has developed its own approach to information literacy, the librarians interviewed for this report do stress some very common themes, among others:

- Build awareness for information literacy, don't be afraid to toot your horn and build allies in the faculty.
- Try to integrate information literacy into the actual curriculum in a formal way if possible
- Information literacy should follow the curriculum and not the other way around
- Information literacy should not be an edict imposed from above but should carefully consider the daily needs of the patron.
- Seek out graduate students with specialized needs; approach them since they will often not approach you.
- Reach out to other college departments for assistance and even instructors when necessary and don't be afraid to ask.
- Be aggressive about using general college introductory events and platforms such as freshman orientation, departmental introductions, and postings on the college web site, and intranet to pursue information literacy objectives
- Assure that the library's educational capabilities are projected through and indeed marketed through campus educational software systems such as Blackboard.
- Develop time saving tutorials or consider using those developed by other colleges
- Inventory, catalog and assess the library educational approaches and capabilities of various libraries and departments –especially important for research universities. However, avoid authoritarian centralization
- Develop a listserv or mailing list for information literacy
- Reach out to key stakeholders and know your allies in the administration, faculty and even the student newspaper.
- Be aware of the ACRL's work on information literacy and develop a plan for meeting its objectives

Seton Hall

COLLEGE DESCRIPTION

Seton Hall is one of the oldest private Catholic universities in the United States, founded in 1856. The University is a Doctoral 2 level Carnegie class institution; it has approximately 10,000 students and offers advanced graduate programs in business, physical therapy, theology, education, nursing, law and diplomacy, among other subjects. Seton Hall also has a well known distance learning program.

Seton Hall, located in northeastern New Jersey, is also noted for its interest in on-campus educational and administrative computing. The College's Teaching Learning Technology Center has joined forces with the college library and other college departments to finance a major effort in enhancing library user education at Seton Hall. We spoke with Beth Bloom, associate professor and reference librarian at Seton Hall.

CLASSES

The library holds 150-180 distinct classes per year in a broad range of subject disciplines. Classes to serve the main freshman English course requirement account for about 40% of the classes offered by the Library; other major areas that require significant input from library educational personnel include business and nursing. In addition to formal classes, the Library pursues the potentially needy patron through a number of virtual channels. "We are also attached to their courses through Blackboard (educational software for traditional and distance class management) so they can contact us for help and we have an email ask-a-librarian service," notes Beth.

According to Ms. Bloom, the academic departments themselves in many ways help determine the library's teaching schedule: "The professors ask for library staff to help them so the professors are a self selecting group -- the only thing that does not fall into that category is the English Department."

MAJOR EFFORT TO DEVELOP WEB-BASED TRAINING

The library received a $75,000 grant from Seton Hall's Teaching Learning Technology Center to finance the initial stages in the development of a broad range of web-based tutorials for the library. The internal grant allows Seton Hall room to experiment without cutting into the library's traditional budget for other pressing items. Initially, the Library is focusing on subject specific tutorials for certain high -volume educational services demand course areas such as Freshman English and Introductory Psychology. It is also developing tutorials for basic library functions such as "Introduction to the Library" and "Use of the Library Catalog". The course-specific library training modules help students to hone in on information resources that can help them in a specific subject area and with specific library skills. The hope is that the emphasis on meeting information needs for important early courses can serve as an early positive reinforcing experience for students. Seton Hall plans to gradually expand the program. "The grant is for 3 years," explained

Ms. Bloom, "but we will continue with the project when the grant runs out. We plan to make these (tutorials) better and to develop others. Probably we will do one in nursing. One of my colleagues has developed something in business."

The library is working closely with Seton Hall's instructional designers to develop sophisticated, appealing but easy to use tutorials that include animation, video and interactive responses to student inquiry. Thus far, the Library has only posted bare-bones versions of the ultimate works to come. "What you have up there now just a basically it goes from one page to the next and asks questions and it gives examples," explains Ms. Bloom.

The project allows the academic computing department to work closely with faculty, enhancing the value of their joint efforts.

STAFFING

The library has 14 full time librarians and all but 2 or 3 participate in instruction. A coordinator and a few others tend to teach somewhat more than the other librarians but the work load appears to be fairly generally spread.

LIBRARY'S EDUCATIONAL LOAD

Educational traffic to the library has been increasing and this was one of the factors in getting the grant for instructional technology.

WEB EDUCATION STRATEGY

Seton Hall tries to steer students towards authoritative web sites and away from general free style web searching. "We try to steer people away from the search engines. They do not know how to use them and the literature shows that they do not know how to use web research. Kids do not know how to evaluate a good site from a bad one. I encourage them to use government resources. We catalog web sites, mostly government resources. Absolutely we have developed a web research guide page in various areas. We encourage them to use the databases which are designed for college use and most of the websites are not and we encourage them to use the resources that we are paying megabucks for."

ADVICE TO OTHER LIBRARIES

Ms. Bloom sums up her advice to other libraries as follows: "I could give a three day lecture. Catalog. Train your students in information literacy. Know what resources they need, know how to evaluate those resources, know what resources suite their need."

Concerning Web-based tutorials: "Know your population and address different learning styles. Start with the person you are developing it for." In other words it is about what they need to know not about what you may enjoy pointing out to them.

Prince George's Community College

COLLEGE DESCRIPTION

Prince George's Community Colleges is a large community college in Maryland with 12,000 full time students and 23,000 part timers. The College has a large distance learning program as well as strong traditional programs in nursing. We spoke with Norma Schmidt, Librarian for Instruction and Reference, Prince George's Community College

BASIC EDUCATIONAL EFFORTS

The library web site offers PowerPoint presentations on a range of introductory library topics such as "The Basics of Boolean Searching". In workshops library instructors refer to the presentations; students can then review them at their own pace. The PowerPoint presentations also cover a few of the most commonly used of the library's 23 major leased databases: Proquest, Infotrac and Literature Resource Center. The Library developed the PowerPoint presentations themselves and did not use an outside vendor or other department of the college for assistance. The Library is currently in the process of developing a tutorial specifically aimed at the College's large body of distance learning students. Many rarely get to campus and need a simple focused tutorial to give them what traditional students get in a required library orientation session.

HEAVIEST USERS OF EDUCATIONAL SERVICES

"English and Psychology are the two biggest users. Both are major courses involving large numbers of students who must do research; indeed, one of the requirements of basic English is to learn to write a research paper."

Approximately 65% of the library's instructional staff time is devoted to students in the basic introductory English class. Psychology classes account for another 15% of the library staff's instructional load; all other classes account for the remaining 20% of instructional time. Other class subject that sometimes require subject specific library instructional services include nursing, speech, history, physical education, chemistry, and computer information studies.

Although the Library does not catalog web sites it does recommend sites as part of its information literacy training, particularly in freshman English. Librarians point students in the direction of dictionary and style guide sites, and sites related to writing improvement.

Most library instruction occurs during the regularly assigned classroom hours for instructors who "book" the library in advance and then take their classes to the library for subject specific library instruction. To some degree, the library staff specializes in particular subject areas. For example, one individual specializes in the social sciences, another in children's literature. While most instruction is for students, the Library will also occasionally hold workshops for faculty, particularly to introduce a new database or other resource.

STAFF TIME DEVOTED TO TRAINING

The Library has 6 full time and 5 part time librarians plus a few student helpers who primarily work on circulation or "in the stacks." At least 2 full time librarians concern themselves primarily with training and "everybody gets involved," at least to some extent. In an average week the library might teach 15 classes with an average class size of about 20.

CHANGE IN THE TEACHING LOAD

The Library's teaching load has remained approximately the same over the past few years.

ADVICE TO OTHER LIBRARIES

Ms. Schmidt advises: "Focus on the student and what they need and don't focus on yourself and what you want to teach."

Bowling Green State University

DESCRIPTION OF THE COLLEGE

Bowling Green State University is a large, public university located in Bowling Green, Ohio with a total student enrollment of approximately 19,000 and with total educational revenues exceeding $250 million from all sources. The college is a doctoral 1 Carnegie class institution with major graduate programs in business, education, American culture studies and many other fields.

LIBRARY TRAINING THROUGH INTRODUCTORY ENGLISH

The Library trains most incoming students through a major introductory English course (dubbed English 112). The course requires a "library component" which is an introduction to the library, and an overview of databases, the library catalog, reference services, circulation and other aspects of the library. The Library has redesigned the library instruction component to make it more "web-based" and students now complete it at their own pace, though it must be completed by the end of the semester in which it is started. The college developed the system in-house.

THE INSTRUCTIONAL LOAD

According to Mr. Chris Miko, Dean of the Library, the Library's instructional load has been increasing and accounts for about a third of the total staff time of the library's professional staff (a figure which excludes time spent in general reference work, some of which is also concerned with general library training). The Library has been using a web-based instructional system for 4 to 5 years.

TIES WITH OTHER ACADEMIC DEPARTMENTS

In order to handle the instructional load, the Library has forged alliances with other departments of the college which both have an interest in information literacy and the resources to make either an independent contribution to library training or a contribution in cooperation with the Library's professional staff. The library has "made connections with our College of Technology and College of Education to teach credit classes at this point, " explains Mr. Miko.

Bowling Green does have a secret weapon in its quest for support. "We have an executive vice president who was the dean of the library at some point - -it really helps to have the upper administration supporting it (information literacy)."

The Library has also developed an array of tutorials to help take pressure off of the instructional and reference staff. "The process can be costly but the results will be worth the price. Creating the class itself is very time consuming on the front end but the end result should be more independent learners in terms of the library," explains Miko.

STAFFING

The Library has a coordinator of user education who more or less works full time on instructional issues, but virtually the entire professional staff is involved in one way or another in education issues. The Library has a 25-person professional staff and all but one or two are involved in training students. In addition, another 25 part timers or students are involved in some fashion. The Library's total number of employees including students and part timers in 120. Individuals working in special collections are particularly likely to be involved in training students.

TRAINING FOR FACULTY AND ADMINISTRATORS

"Not a whole lot here at Bowling Green. When we have tried it in the past it has not really been utilized. I think what each university tries to capitalize on is their unique strengths -- our special collections are our music and popular culture collections so we make sure that those resources are "out there."

ADVICE TO OTHER LIBRARIES

Mr. Miko is skeptical of the one size fits all-all at once philosophy of training students to use library resources. He notes: "At this point I still question the "English 112" orientation -- I question that approach - in terms of how relevant it is to the students -- at that point they really may not really need it. When you really need to know the material and resources -- it is at the point of learning. We should put our resources more into when they actually need the library -- that is when you hit them."

Polytechnic University

COLLEGE DESCRIPTION

Polytechnic University is a small but prominent engineering-oriented research university with a total FTE enrollment of about 2500, located in Brooklyn, New York.. The University is perhaps best known for its chemical and other engineering programs. Generous gifts from alumni have recently enabled it to finance college/library technology programs that are on the wish lists of many colleges similar in size and scope. Since the present at Polytechnic University is likely to be the near future for many other small and medium sized colleges, we decided to take a look at how Polytechnic trains its students in library technologies and information literacy. We interviewed Jana Richman, Director of Library Services.

CLASSES FOR FRESHMEN

Polytechnic requires freshman (though not graduate students or transfers) to take a short two hour non-credit introductory course about the library, which they take in the first semester of the first year. Library staff divide the freshman class into groups of 30 and conduct the two-hour class with each group. Prior to the class, at freshman orientation, the new students receive a general introduction to the library and its resources, which serves as basic preparation for the more focused two-hour class in the first semester.

Since Polytechnic is part of a consortium of academic libraries in Brooklyn that includes seven other local colleges, the introductory course also mentions some of the library facilities of these other member institutions (Pratt Institute, St Francis, St Joseph, Brooklyn College, Long Island University, Medger Evers, and NYC Technical College).

ONLINE GUIDES

Polytechnic has developed a range of online guides to introduce and train its students in the Library's resources. "We did it ourselves in-house," says Ms. Richman, responding to our question of whether she outsources development of online tools explaining the use of library resources. "We do everything inside of the library. I have a web team that includes someone who does the design, and the video. I had library staff participating and that was that. We are using Real Player. A lot of our resources are now available on the web and we use it as a very important aspect of information literacy -- providing catalog, training, workshops, multi-media lab -- document delivery online -- and reference chat through Liveperson." Polytechnic's library guides can be accessed at:

HTTP://Library.poly.edu

STAFF

The Library has a staff of 13: 6 librarians, 3 support staff, 2 "techies", and 1 web designer and 1 information technology instruction specialist.

COURSES

The library offers 23 courses per month in a broad range of subjects. Says Jana: "They are aimed at anybody at Poly who wants to take them and they are not only how to use libraries but they are also in subjects such as Excel Basics, Basic HTML and Web Page Development, Posting Documents in BLACKBOARD, How to Create Presentations in PowerPoint, Using The Online Databases, Using Microsoft Publisher, etc."

Up until now the library staff itself has done virtually all of the teaching but his may change a bit in the future. "I have started to explore the possibility of other departments helping us out so if there is someone who is a whiz at HTML, and my staff does not have that skill, then I will invite them to teach a workshop. It is good for their resume. I even use students to help us out."

THE PROACTIVE APPROACH

Polytechnic Librarians are also invited into classrooms to give demonstrations, often on how to find library resource in specific subject areas. Polytechnic is a completely wireless environment so the librarians show up with laptops and give demonstrations on the spot. In addition, the librarians prowl the hallways and floors of the Library so they can be available to students "on demand." Ms. Richman explains: "We don't do just the standard bibliographic instruction; we do a lot of "just in time" and take an "on demand" approach to information literacy. We don't have as many librarians standing at the service desk. We have more students doing that; we have librarians really doing librarian's work."

FACILITIES

For in-library courses the Library has one large seminar room that can accommodate 25 and another room for 8-10 students "We like that room because we have computers in it."

DETERMINING SPECIALIZED TRAINING NEEDS

Throughout our interview, Ms. Richman stressed the importance of frequent and direct contact with library end users and advised aggressively seeking out their specific needs. Polytechnic has eight major academic departments and the Library has nine subject specialists that roughly correspond to these departments; these specialists are responsible for providing a web page that has links to databases and other reference materials for the specific departments. Each subject specialist is a liaison to their assigned department, and the specialists become valuable eyes and ears in determining specialized library training needs.

The nine areas for which Polytechnic has subject specialists are Chemistry, Chemical Engineering & Material Science, Civil and Environmental, Computer & Information Science (Programming), Electrical & Computer (networks), Humanities and Social

Science, Management, Mathematics Mechanical Aerospace and Manufacturing Engineering, and Physics.

DISTANCE LEARNING & OUTLYING CAMPUSES

Polytechnic has struggled with the issue of providing library education services to satellite campuses and distance learning students. The college has two campuses that do not have their own libraries. Although these entities are not far from the main campus, and are located in New York City's surrounding suburbs, students at these centers, often graduate students, do not often have the time to do their research at the main library in Brooklyn. In addition to serving the suburban campuses, the main library also sends its emissaries to next door Manhattan to conduct library use seminars at an outlying facility.

Ironically, since the graduate students may not have had a basic information literacy course, they are often less able than undergraduates to conduct research and intelligently exploit all the resources available to them. Jana comments that: "We find that many of the graduate students have problems particularly with searching databases. I think that our graduate students - they are particular-- database searching is not easy and I don't think many of them know how to do it - but they are not easy to catch them -- they are not organized or accessible -- it is hard to make an organized effort one with this professor and two with that professor."

THE IMPACT OF THE WIRELESS ENVIRONMENT

Polytechnic has a broad-based wireless network and requires students to own laptops. The ample wireless network combined with a student body equipped with mobile computing and communications devices makes Polytechnic an interesting laboratory in which to examine the academic library in the heralded soon-to-arrive wireless campus environment. Only a few colleges now have such network/hardware combinations; however, ten years from today most colleges may be in a situation similar to Polytechnic's situation today. The impact on Polytechnic's academic library is startling: rather than decreasing library use by students and faculty, as many had predicted, the wireless environment seems to encourage physical visits to the library, at least in this academic setting. Ms. Richman comments:

"We keep track of how many students come into the library -- I was amazed -- our numbers are increasing. I am not clear what it is but the increase is enormous over the past 2 years. The wireless network allows the student to work anywhere in the library; they can sit comfortably in a couch and work, they can be in a study group and they can work. Wireless liberates them; it gives them a huge amount of opportunity. My students they are now sitting in the stacks with their laptops, they are in group study working on their research projects; they use the library for studying whether in groups or individually."

ONE ON ONE TUTORIALS

Polytechnic has developed a series of one on one tutorials that students can access via the internet. Typical tutorials include RESEARCH BLUEPRINT; a basic tutorial designed to teach undergraduates how to do basic library research. Another aimed largely at graduate students is titled, simply: HOW TO DO YOUR DISSERTATION. The tutorials are developed by library staff and often are done in the program FLASH. Although the tutorials can take 150-250 librarian man-hours to create they tend to save money in the long run by liberating staff time, since the tutorials answer many questions that otherwise would have to be answered by library staff. The Library is also not shy about seeking help from talented students in giving informal tutorials to their peers or in working on website tutorial projects.

Richman points out: "We have so much talent here we very often ask students help us out -- in the long run it is pretty cheap (to develop the tutorials)."

ADVICE FOR OTHER LIBRARIES

Ms. Richman advises her fellow academic librarians to view library training as an emerging field that has put academic librarians on the same status footing as faculty. She notes: "Instruction has become one of the most important facets of academic library work. It really made us peers with faculty; in the past we were like a warehouse with books, now we are much more a part of the educational process, but it also requires different skills. You have to constantly upgrade your own skills. I have just learned

Microsoft Publisher. Don't assume that since you are in cataloging today you will not be in reference tomorrow."

William H. Welch Medical Library of the Johns Hopkins University

DESCRIPTION

The Johns Hopkins University is one of the premier research universities in the United States with particularly strong programs in the health sciences. Hopkins generally receives more research grants and spends more on scientific research than any other private university in the United States. The William H. Welch Medical Library of the Johns Hopkins University serves the University's School of Medicine, the Bloomberg School of Public Health, the Johns Hopkins Hospital, and the School of Nursing -- a total end user population of more than 10,000. Medical libraries have difficult and unique information literacy needs; to understand Hopkins' approach we spoke with Jayne Campbell, Associate Director for Information Services and Education.

OVERALL STAFF LIBRARY

The Library employs approximately 80 FTE including librarians and support staff; the Library does not employ student workers. Thirteen librarians are devoted largely to instruction as their major task.

REQUIRED COURSES

The various health-related professional schools do not require any information science training at this time. However, the Library has an active program of regular courses for those that seek out information literacy training, and a large array of non-credit courses offered in practical information technology skills. The basic "hand-on" library 101 course is offered in the Spring and Fall, and small classes (maximum 12) guarantee individual attention; however, only a tiny fraction of incoming students take the class.

Most information literacy training done in this time-stretched and demanding environment is done on an "as needed" basis. The Library imparts many skills through brief but highly focused workshops and short classes, which emphasize immediate strategies to solve pressing problems.

Campbell explains that information training in a research hospital environment is very much driven by the frenetic pace and demanding nature of the tasks at hand: "It is possible that individual course directors will make information literacy some kind of regular component of their course. Part of that is the curriculum is packed as it is. They (doctors) are very oriented towards what they need at that moment. The School of Nursing has been somewhat more open to having their students receive instruction from the Library and are willing to incorporate it into their curriculums."

ONLINE TUTORIALS

To supplement classes and seminars the Library is developing a series of E-learning pages on its web site. The tutorials are being developed in house by the Library's Advanced Technology Group, which includes programmers, web designers, and graphic artists -- about fourteen total professional staff members. "Our goal is to develop some kind of tutorial for each one of the classes that we offer in our program."

Some tutorials under development include: "Resources for PDA" (personal digital assistant), "Course Evaluation", "Patient Tracking", "Use of PubMed", and "Staying Current with Research," a guide for doctors, scholars and others that need to stay current with a certain body of medical research. At present the tutorials are not interactive and creating them takes only about 10-20 hours of an instructors time, apart from the time spent by the Advanced Technology Group. Each tutorial, shorn of bells and whistles, and sharing a common interface and "look" can be quickly and efficiently developed as needed. "The tutorials will pretty closely mirror what we offer in the classroom hours," says Ms. Campbell.

Fancier offerings may be on the horizon. "These are text-based but we are talking about the next set that we might begin to work on and there is some possibility that they will be interactive."

SEARCH STRATEGIES

One of the major issues in physician information literacy has been: does a hospital want doctors whose time may be worth hundreds of dollars per hour spending a lot of personal time searching the internet for information? Is this a waste of money when this might be done just as effectively by a librarian or even a graduate student commanding a much lower salary and able to liberate a doctor's time?

Comments Campbell: "We take two approaches. There is and there will always be a group of physicians who are willing and able to do the searches themselves. For the others the physicians here tend to do the searches at the time of need - they tend not to take the time to get help."

One long-term approach, not yet completely successful at Hopkins, is to make the librarian an actual part of the clinical team in casework, along with the usual array of doctors, nurses and others such as nutritionists, counselors and medical technicians. Campbell explains her thinking:

"We want the librarians to become part of the clinical team. We have a program in place where each one of the librarians is trying to be a liaison to a department and we are hoping that through the liaison contacts that -- as the relationships develop -- the librarian will show that there is value in him or her becoming part of the team. It is a great challenge to make them see that there is value in the information that we provide. It is difficult to prove to them that it has impact on the clinical outcome. Vanderbilt University Medical School has some pretty good examples of some ways that those programs can be successful."

DISTANCE LEARNING

The Bloomberg School of Public Health has a distance learning program and the Welch Library provides some instruction to some of their students. Says Ms. Campbell: "They will have seminars once in a while that are transmitted to the off-campus students. And they are required to spend some time on campus and we provide some on campus instruction at that time."

NON-REQUIRED AND FEE-BASED COURSES

"The majority of our instruction takes place in forums outside of the academic programs. We have an extensive education program that are available to any faculty, staff or student in the university," notes Ms. Campbell. Some of these require an additional fee. The Library offers more than 200 distinct classes annually in topics such as Microsoft Word, Excel, Access, PowerPoint, and PhotoShop, and in themes such as: "How to Search the Web Effectively" or "Elements of Web Interface Design." Some courses are offered to the public at large although it is rare that people attend from outside the college. Classes that focus on library resources and services are taught by library staff while outside vendors provide instructors for specialized applications. The Library cooperates with the

Office of Continuing Education in sponsoring and marketing these classes and the Library receives 80% of the tuition money for the courses that require a fee.

ADVICE FOR OTHER LIBRARIES

Ms. Campbell emphasizes two points: pay attention to the needs of your end users and pay attention to what they are doing with their research.

"It is really very important to pay attention to what your users tell you that they need. We could have a program that we think is fantastic but if it doesn't meet their needs it isn't really (a good program). Just because we do something well it doesn't mean that we are meeting the needs of our users."

In advanced medical research centers, tenure and promotion decisions are dramatically impacted not only by publication, but also by participation in and presentations at medical meetings. Consequently, to a greater extent than in other academic disciplines, medical professionals need presentation skills as part of their library information literacy training.

The need to present extensive documentation and sources and to generate sophisticated and appealing graphs, charts and the general quantitative "aplomb" typical of many medical/pharmaceutical meetings has been incorporated into the literacy approach taken by the University.

Ms. Campbell comments: "Look at what they are doing downstream with the information. I think that our program has been put in place to address as many areas of the scientific communication process as we can . We help them write a manuscript or develop a bibliography - they need to do something with that - present it at a seminar, write a grant proposal." In the end it is not surprising that medical writing is such a major business in the United States and has sprung up as a way to help physicians and other scientifically oriented healthcare professionals to get their point across in an often-contentious medical environment. Information literacy in the hospital/healthcare setting must also take these needs into account.

Temple University

COLLEGE DESCRIPTION

Temple is one of three major public research universities in Pennsylvania with more than 30,000 total students. Temple offers more than 58 doctoral degrees and 6 professional degree and is perhaps best known for its healthcare-related graduate and professional degree programs. Temple was a private university until 1965 when it became affiliated with the State of Pennsylvania. We spoke with Boris Teske, Library User Education Program Leader, of the main Samual S. Paley Library and affiliated libraries of Temple University.

Temple currently must meet self-described modest information literacy requirements as part of a state-mandated core curriculum. Students generally meet the requirements by completing online tutorials which are restricted to staff and students of the University. These tutorials mirror paper workbooks that had been previously used by the library to accomplish the same purpose. The tutorial covers basic library skills such as identifying and interpreting records, locating books by call number, finding electronic texts, using online periodical indices, and other basic library and research functions.

"Students take about an hour to complete it," explains Mr. Teske who is quick to add that the University is revising the tutorials.

NEW INFORMATION LITERACY REQUIREMENTS

In the recent past, Temple's information literacy education efforts have been relatively modest but Mr. Teske believes that change is coming soon. The Library expects more stringent information literacy requirements in the near future as Pennsylvania state education officials start to stress the issue more than in the past. Accreditation agencies are also beginning to stress information literacy, notes Teske, and he expects this also to be a catalyst for the development of increasingly stringent information literacy requirements at Temple. The college will also probably adopt a new core curriculum, possibly as early as 2004 (although no absolutely firm dates have been announced), and the Library is expecting this to impact information literacy. The increasing emphasis in higher education on educational outcomes assessment, Teske believes, is a force driving curriculum reform and, ultimately, information literacy as well.

ONLINE TUTORIALS

In preparation for this eventuality, the college library started to examine various options for upgrading their library skills tutorials. Budget constraints encouraged the library to look at publicly available offerings from colleges nationwide. After some searching and experimentation, Temple decided to use TILT – the Texas Information Literacy Tutorial – which had been made available to the academic community by the University of Texas as an open source solution. Temple is revising TILT to suit its specific needs. "A library like ours is able to request to use and modify this product as long as we acknowledge the originator," says Teske.

Temple librarians were impressed by TILT's "quizzing" features and other interactive functions and by its visual appeal. Another factor in choosing TILT was its wide availability throughout the academic library community. "And even though it was written in the late 1990's it is quite close to the 2000 ACRL standards," enthuses Mr. Teske. Through TILT, Temple librarians will not only be able to present a suitable information literacy program to students, but also track their progress in mastering that program, and alert professors or librarians to their progress.

"We are trying very much to bring us in line with the ACRL (Association of College and Research Libraries) information literacy competency standards for higher education. In general, Teske expects TILT to be a big help in meeting these standards. The more sophisticated online tutorials will supplement but not supplant Temple's traditional efforts. "We have for quite some time done the course related instruction - -that is our 'bread an butter'," notes Mr. Teske.

However, Mr. Teske seems disappointed in the "grab em while you can in Freshman English" approach to information literacy training. Library orientations, while helpful, are also deficient.

"We do have some luck with our pre-semester orientations at the graduate level but (for undergraduates) it seems to be a missed opportunity. It is left to freshman seminar. I suppose what we really have been doing is waiting for the existing first year writing and other core courses to pick up the slack; it is an imperfect system -- that is why I am excited about the prospects for the new core curriculum."

TILT TOWARDS TEXAS

"We looked at various tutorials to get a sense as to what had been done. We were looking at some others. Our favorite site was to go to CUNY (City University of New York) - someone had collated some of the better tutorials." Another tutorial that Temple considered was: "Go for the Gold" developed by James Madison University. The tutorials and associated url's collected by CUNY are presented below.

Information Literacy Tutorial
University of Wisconsin Parkside
http://www.uwp.edu/library/
Go For The Gold
James Madison University
http://library.jmu.edu/library/gold/modules.htm
Library Research Tutorial
An Information Literacy Skills Program
Griffith University Queensland Australia
http://www4.gu.edu.au/shr/lrt/
Online Tutorials
Ball State University Libraries
http://www.bsu.edu/library/services/is/tutorials.html
ViRGiL - Virtual Research Guide to Information Literacy
Westchester Community College - SUNY
http://www.sunywcc.edu/library/tutorial/index11.htm

Information Literacy Tutorial
Minneapolis Community & Technical College
http://www.mctc.mnscu.edu/academicAffairs/library/tutorials/in
folit/
Library Skills Tutorial
Grand Valley State University
http://www.gvsu.edu/library/webtutor/title&tc.htm
Library Web Tutorial
George Mason University
http://library.gmu.edu/training/webtut/

THE USER EDUCATION COMMITTEE

The Library has a User Education Committee that makes policy on instruction-related issues. The seven member panel includes instructional librarians, administrators and program heads. This group will have a great deal of input in developing the Library's new approach to information literacy, but the Library has also reached out to non-library faculty and other stakeholders. The User Education Committee sent out a query to various library subject specialists asking them which college departments were most interested in information literacy, and which faculty members are teaching these skills in the context of non-library science courses. The major reason for the query was to define what is happening in the university on an ad hoc basis in terms of information literacy teaching, and who might be likely users/supporters of information literacy training.

CLASSROOM FACILITIES

The Library has a "modest wired classroom here in the library" but tends to use the University's Tuttleman Learning Center "which is very well equipped with multiple smart classrooms and computer labs." Mr. Teske notes that the Library is generally "able to reserve that for library instruction (by and large we get what we need) we are able to give overhead demonstrations and at very best we have a workstation for each student but this varies on need and the availability of rooms."

PARTNERSHIPS WITH STAKEHOLDERS

Teske is not worried about adequate facilities but does yearn for a set of partnerships with stakeholders in information literacy: students, professors and department chairman, among others.

"Information literacy is a very specific thing and librarians offering sessions is not getting that done. To develop something like that requires that it be developed with faculty. At the moment the area we are making progress is in the basic area -- offerings of traditional library instruction go on across the board. We do reach in a piecemeal fashion various stakeholders but we do not have the strategic partnerships in place."

University At Albany, State University Of New York

COLLEGE DESCRIPTION

The University at Albany is one of the four main research centers sponsored by the State University of New York System (SUNY). The University has an FTE enrollment of approximately 17,000 and advanced professional schools in criminal justice, social welfare, public policy and information science, among other areas. The University at Albany is the site of SUNY's flagship school of library science, and also a leader in the SUNY-wide movement to enhance information literacy and better integrate it into the overall SUNY academic program. We spoke with Trudi Jacobson, Coordinator of User Education Programs at the University at Albany.

SUNY INFORMATION LITERACY REQUIRMENT

The information literacy requirements at U Albany are imposed by the State University of New York system and all colleges under the SUNY rubric must meet the requirement, though the colleges are given considerable latitude in how they go about doing this. SUNY trustees developed the information literacy requirement, initially called Information Management, on a competency model and not on a course model. The objective it for students to demonstrate competency, not merely mechanically complete course requirements. "Some SUNY colleges may still be doing it the traditional way, through the freshman English course," notes Ms. Jacobson, "and each college has to submit to the (SUNY central administration) Board of Trustees a plan on how they are going to do this."

REQUIRED COURSES

SUNY requires one course to fulfill the system-wide information literacy requirement, which may be fulfilled by a one or three credit course. The requirement must be fulfilled in the first or second year of an incoming freshman student's tenure at the University, and the Library has developed an array of courses that will satisfy the requirement.

Trudi explains: "There are about 8-10 courses that would fulfill the requirement. (Students must take one of them) There are two that are somewhat generic. They are: INFORMATION LITERACY (1 credit, 1 quarter course -- meets two hours per week for 7 weeks) the University offers 40 sections and the enrollment maximum is twenty three."

The University at Albany also offers a second one credit course similar to the main course but with a greater emphasis on the sciences. The Library offers only 4 sections of this course, but offers 36 sections of the basic course without the scientific accent.

CONTENTS OF THE MAIN COURSE

The one credit information literacy course covers a broad range of topics and is not restricted to the nuts and bolts of database searching and "where can you find this?" type information that weighs down some basic library science courses.

Ms. Jacobson explains: "They learn a variety of research skills and concepts about information so that it is not entirely skill-based. They are being taught concepts. They get a sense of information in today's world: social and ethical issue , plagiarism, copyright, privacy issues, digital divide , primary and secondary sources, the flow of information. We find a large difference between the students that have taken this course and those who are just getting a class or two in a particular course . They seem to be much better prepared and some faculty members have begun to notice the difference in how students do research."

STAFF

When the University instituted its information literacy requirements it gave the Library two additional full time equivalent staff lines. The lines were made available for either reference or instruction but the Library has largely used them for instruction.

The Library has a staff of approximately 40 librarians; approximately 10 librarians teach in one of the 2 main courses that satisfy the information literacy requirement for most students; about ten librarians teach in course-related instruction in specific library science areas.

CLASSROOM TECHNOLOLGY

The University at Albany invested in a high tech classroom specially designed for training in information literacy and equipped it with 23 student workstations, an instructor workstation, 2 large screens at either end of the room for projecting materials, a document camera, video systems and a Robotel. The Robotel allows the instructors to take control of the student's workstation. "We can send an image and keyboard control to a particular student." enthused Trudi. Frequently, if students are doing work and they have found a great database they can show it on the other screens. If students are not paying attention we can take control of their keyboard. This is why we originally got it but now we are using it for loftier pedagogical purposes," says Ms. Jacobson, not entirely tongue in cheek.

The Robotel includes both hardware and software and the library shared its acquisition cost with a special campus program to finance "smart" classrooms. The Robotel is linked to each computer in the room, giving the instructor extensive control. The University at Albany has had the Robotel for 2 years, having acquired it in the Spring semester of 2000.

STRESS ON EVALUTION

The U at Albany information literacy approach encourages students to acquire the needed tools to evaluate web sites and other information sources.

"We do a lot with teaching them how to be effective searchers - how to use quote marks - - and we spend a good time in each course on how to evaluate what they find. They do some practicing with evaluation. For example, as an exercise they are presented with three web sites – one is biased, one is scholarly and one is a joke site -- and students have to answer questions about how to evaluate the sites and they must do an annotated bibliography for each course."

OTHER COURSES THAT FULFILL THE INFORMATION LITERACY REQUIREMENT

One interesting aspect of the University at Albany program is that the University has integrated an information literacy agenda into a select number of courses in other disciplines. The completion of one of these courses serves to fulfill the information literacy requirement.

However, instructors in these courses follow guidelines and teach info lit concepts to a greater extent than they have typically been taught in "English 101" type courses or at least are used as a kind of back door by academic libraries to "sneak in" library research skills into lessons on writing a research paper.

Some of the courses that satisfy the basic information literacy requirement at U Albany are:

INTERNET AND INFORMATION ACCESS – This is a course aimed primarily at information science students and those in related disciplines. It draws an enrollment of about 400 students and is a semester long 3-credit course.

INTRODUCTORY LINGUISTICS – This course is designed largely for linguistics majors and it imparts basic information science concepts as well as information designed particularly for linguistics students. Another information science course that satisfies the info literacy requirement -- THE INFORMATION ENVIRONMENT -- is a 3-credit course that largely draws information science majors. It focuses particularly on web development and typically draws about 60 students.

CHINA IN THE POST UTOPIAN AGE- This geography course is actually taught by the Library's subject specialist for geography.

EAST ASIAN RESEARCH AND BIBLIOGRAPHIC METHODS - - This course is modeled in part on the 1-credit course that meets the info literacy requirement- UNL205 –but is specifically adjusted for students studying in Japanese, Korean or Chinese.

Some additional courses that have adjusted their program to meet the information literacy requirement include CLASSISM, RACISM AND SEXISM (woman's studies), and PRINCIPALS OF CAREER AND LIFE PLANNING (Educational Psychology).

PROCESS THAT A PROFESSOR GOES THROUGH TO CERTIFY A COURSE

Faculty members that are interested in qualifying their courses to meet the college information literacy requirement initially apply by filling out a form and submitting it to a small committee composed of 2 librarians and 3-4 non-library-science faculty members. Courses that meet the requirements have an extra selling point with students.

ONLINE TUTORIALS

The Library has developed 4 major tutorials, some of which are used by libraries across the country at no fee. One of the tutorials teaches the evaluation of internet sites. The URL to access the tutorials is: **library.albany.edu/usered/tut.html**. Other tutorials include a virtual tour of the main library and a tutorial on recognizing and avoiding plagiarism. The tutorials serve as a tool for instructors in non-library science courses that have been certified by the Library for fulfilling the information literacy requirement. The instructors of these courses refer their students to the tutorials which are set up in such a way so that the Library can inform the faculty member when one of their students has completed the tutorial. This gives the Library at least some input into the non-library science course that nonetheless meets the information literacy requirement and assures that certain basic tenets are covered. "The tutorials are heavily used by each of the courses that satisfy the requirements," notes Trudi.

COST OF DEVELOPING THE TUTORIALS

The Library developed its own tutorials without outside assistance. "We have one librarian responsible for developing them. I would say it took (for each tutorial) maybe about 30% of her time for 3 months or our grad student took most of her time for 6 months at 10 hours per week. We find it pays off. At Albany about 1500 students per month are using them."

Also, many of these students use more than one tutorial so total usage of tutorials per month significantly exceeds this figure. Indeed, the average number of tutorials used per student is two. SUNY Albany's numbers in this respect are higher than most comparable figures that we have seen; however, SUNY Albany has taken many measures to integrate the tutorials into the actual curriculum and not just the library science curriculum. Instructors in the main 1-credit library science courses that satisfy the information literacy requirement do not necessarily use the tutorials but may prefer to teach the same materials in their own way. The Library has no plans to develop new, full fledged interactive tutorials in the near future but it is planning two smaller tutorials, one on primary Vs secondary materials, and another on scholarly Vs. popular materials.

IMPACT ON TRENDS IN INSTRUCTION

Since the information literacy program better prepares students to use the library, the student appetite for further instruction tends to be greater than in the past. Library instruction at U of Albany encourages subject specialists librarians to reach out to upper level undergraduates and graduate students and better familiarize them with the subject specific resources that might not have been completely covered in introductory courses and tutorials. "Now that the students have the basics the subject specialists can work on refining that knowledge," explains Ms. Jacobson.

ADVICE TO OTHER LIBRARIES

"We have found that it is immensely pleasurable to do the main information science course - having a chance to work with students on a continuing basis is immensely rewarding and we are seeing much greater results than we had seen before with the course-related instruction. The student are really 'getting it' because they are really being exposed in a concentrated way."

University of Illinois at Urbana-Champaign

COLLEGE DESCRIPTION

The University of Illinois at Urbana-Champaign is a major research university with more than 35,000 full time students, the University's library complex encompasses more than 42 separate libraries housed in 20 distinct buildings with a cumulative library staff of 126 librarians, a support staff of 222 and 124 student assistants. In addition, Urbana-Champaign offers a highly ranked graduate library science program.

COORDINATION OF DIVERSITY

Urbana-Champaign has traditionally taken a highly decentralized view of information literacy training and allowed its various library units to develop approaches thought most suitable to their particular patron and student base. Although this view has not fundamentally changed, the University has decided to bring greater coordination to its efforts and, as part of this effort, recently created the position of Coordinator for Information Literacy Services and Instruction. We spoke with Lisa Janicke Hinchliffe, who now holds this newly created position.

EMERGING DISCIPLINES

One leading area of focus for the new coordination effort will be identifying and developing library training strategies for emerging academic disciplines, especially those that cut across traditional discipline distinctions. Hinchliffe notes that disciplines that emerged over the past 20 years such as Women's Studies, Environmental Studies, and more recently – Biotechnology – have not always had the benefit of library subject specialists, bibliographies and online tutorials focused on their distinct curriculum. The dearth of proper library support can retard scholarship in emerging disciplines and impact their standing in the academic hierarchy. Hinchliffe hopes that Urbana-Champaign will be able to identify these disciplines, and develop library training and support strategies that help them grow as disciplines and enhance the success of Urbana-Champaign students and faculty in them.

"Biotechnology is a good example," notes Ms. Hinchliffe, "We do not have a biotechnology library but we do have a biotechnology librarian." Biotechnology cuts across various disciplines including business, biology, engineering and environmental science; a campus with a library focused on this emerging discipline will be better placed to educate students and to attract scholars, research grants and positive media and peer attention.

Although Hinchliffe did not emphasize this competitive aspect in our interview, the reality is that library services particularly focused on emerging disciplines can help to attract students and faculties in disciplines that have not always enjoyed such support, and which may be struggling to win academic acceptance.

NOT A DEPARTURE FROM DECENTRALIZATION

Hinchliffe emphasizes that coordination does not mean centralization or standardization.

"Students here can fulfill general education requirements in a great variety of ways so the Library attempts to respond to those various cirricular structures in a way that makes sense for them. We do not have a one size fits all model," says Hinchliffe.

According to Hinchliffe, just about every species of information literacy animal can be found somewhere in the veritable rain forest of library instruction at Urbana, including online tutorials, in-library and in-class training, formal info literacy requirements, one-on-one tutorials and other approaches.

"Historically the University library has had a number of activities done on the unit level; the undergraduate library has done instructional programming for undergraduate first year students. At different points in time we have done that through training TA's in speech communication (the major communication arts course given to incoming freshmen). We give them training in one of the 7 or 8 ways that first year students can fulfill their basic composition requirement. There are alternate ways for students who are – say ESL students – and some test out of that requirement. We have also used online tutorials very extensively."

The State of Illinois does not have a specific information literacy requirement and has left it up to the individual state colleges to develop their own approach. This has the advantage of allowing library educators to follow the curriculum and shape their efforts to the discipline at hand. However, it can also lead to some atomization, duplication of effort and parochialism. At a major research university such as The University of Illinois at Champaign-Urbana, literally hundreds of professionals – professors, librarians, web designers and other technical support staff – will be involved in library education efforts. Coordination of their efforts and cooperation with one another can generate new ideas, lead to the widespread dissemination and adoption of the best ideas, and the gradual weeding out of less successful approaches. Through brown bag lunches, guest speakers and in-house lecturers, and other activities that ease communication among the many interested stakeholders in the library education community, Hinchliffe hopes to promote a cooperative and learning culture.

CAMPUS ADVOCATE

In many ways, library education is unlike any other education discipline at a university. Everyone needs to know how to use the library; it belongs to everyone yet has no champion. Explains Hinchliffe: "We have many libraries doing very good work for their populations. We have not had a campus wide strategy for focusing our efforts; my position is an attempt to create that position – someone who can be a champion of this issue with our campus constituents."

ONLINE TUTORIALS

The University has a vast number of tutorials and each library develops its own. The library systems unit is available to assist individual libraries with technical expertise. In terms of general tutorials online for undergraduates the Library offers a tour of the undergraduate library, and a tutorial on evaluating web sites, among others. The Library is currently re-developing its online tutorial on use of the online catalog tutorial, which itself was recently significantly altered.

Some subject specific university libraries have tutorials on key databases in their subject areas but most tutorials show how to use a range of databases. The development of tutorials follows campus curriculum developments.

"Our development is being driven by the curriculum development on the campus – those are the activities that we are beginning – these are the processes that we are working on right now."

USER EDUCATION COMMITTEE

Hinfliche is meeting with the individual members of the Library's User Education Committee, querying them about what they might like to be offering their patrons, in much the same way that corporate knowledge management officers survey key information users to determine their needs and strengths.

"I am meeting with each unit library for discussion to talk about what they have and what they might like to be offering. The user education committee is working on a process that will feed into our library strategic planning process."

The User Education Committee is composed of librarians and staff members from the various libraries. Its role is to help facilitate some of the policy making and to make recommendations to the larger library about policy.

INSTRUCTIONAL LOAD

Since 1995 the Library has given 900 to 1200 educational presentations per year and the load has not steadily increased or decreased..

THE LIBRARY'S STANDING IN THE COURSE MANAGEMENT SYSTEMS

One issue of pressing concern to Hinchliffe is how the Library will be presented in the University's courseware management system. These ubiquitous systems have become prime vehicles for reaching students and Hinchliffe wants to be assured that the Library and its training resources can be adequately publicized and to some degree made available through the course management system. Consequently, the Library is pursuing discussions with the college's IT Department to develop a suitable approach.

"We are engaged in pursuing partnerships with them," says Hinchliffe, "We use Blackboard and Web CT. The campus is going through an RFP to choose one of the two

– we need a strategy to embed the library's resources within the learning management system."

ADVICE TO OTHER LIBRARIES

- "Effective information literacy programs are embedded in and responsive to the university's curriculum. It needs to be hooked into that curriculum."

- "To me it is not enough to just think about English 101. We really need to look at a whole program of study that a student takes. We need to look at information literacy relative to that whole program of study."

- "On a more practical note: Find out who your strong allies are."

The University Of Toronto

DESCRIPTION OF THE UNIVERSITY

The University of Toronto is a major research university that attracts approximately $200 million (US) annually in grant support and has more than 55,000 full time students and graduate or professional programs in a plethora of disciplines including medicine, engineering, law, business and education, among others. The University's library system includes 32 separate libraries housed on the main campus, subsidiary campuses in suburban Toronto and outlets in related institutions such as research centers and museums. We spoke with Jennifer Mendelsohn, Head of the Reference Department, Robarts Library, the Humanities and Social Science Library at the University of Toronto, and with Jeff Newman., Coordinator of Undergraduate Library Instruction at Robarts.

COORDINATION

In terms of holdings, the University of Toronto (UT) library is one of five largest in North America and the breadth and complexity of its offerings and patron base argues against any kind of highly centralized instructional agenda. Each library forges its own approach to information literacy. Explains Mendelsohn: "We have the independence to do what we need to do; in the science library, for example, they are constantly trying new ideas; we need the flexibility more than centralization."

Newman adds: "Our library system is very much structured so that the library appeals to a particular clientele; they each are in a position to create a customized program."

Although they eschew anything with the clear scent of authoritarian centralization, Mendelsohn and Newman emphasize that UT 's approach to information literacy includes a good deal of information sharing and dissemination of new ideas in a small but communicative community of librarians entrusted with primary educational responsibilities. These librarians, along with some technicians highly involved in library educational processes, have an internal 50-member listserv/mailing list on instructional issues. Ideas are also shared through a 32-member Library Instruction Committee, with representatives from all of UT's member libraries; the Committee meets once per month.

On the provincial level, academic librarians with significant responsibilities for library instruction meet once a year at a university in Toronto (the province's colleges and universities host the conference on a rotating basis) for a three-day conference on instructional issues. ACRL and the CLA also hold library instruction conferences in Ontario.

ONLINE TUTORIALS

On the whole UT has not made a major push into online tutorials. The University Medical Library has online tutorials for basic training in how to conduct a search and how to use a few of the major databases such as Medline. These are largely done in FLASH. The education library is currently developed streaming video for library training but "beyond that there hasn't been a big push for the development of online tutorials."

INTEGRATION OF INFORMATION LITERACY TRAINING INTO MAINSTREAM CLASSES

Up to this point, most information literacy training at UT has been done either on an "as-needed" on demand basis, or through the training of Teaching Assistants in information literacy who would then relay the concepts to their students. Instructors requested that librarians come into their classes and give demonstrations or lectures, often focusing on the information resources available in a particular field of interest. Unlike most colleges in the United States, UT does not require a basic English composition course, and consequently has no ready made vehicle through which to introduce basic research concepts. Nonetheless, UT has found other means that parallel the efforts made by American colleges in the typical "English 101" class.

The University has a large medical program, with a broad range of graduate and professional medical programs, so its basic biology course (dubbed BIO 150) has become a vehicle for introducing science-oriented information literacy concepts to its largely freshman audience. The class has a library instruction module in the class as well as information tool online tutorials specifically designed for that class. However, unlike at many American universities which, oddly enough, emphasize information literacy more to undergraduates than graduate students, "the focus on information literacy does not happen until the graduate level at the University of Toronto," says Newman.

CLASSES OFFERED BY THE LIBRARY

In 2001-02 the entire UT Library system ran 1,613 classes attended by 24,643 participants. The classes might be classified into three groups: those offered by the traditional faculties as traditional for credit courses with some library instructional training, those offered directly by the Library and those offered by the Center for Academic Technology. This center offers courses aimed mostly at instructors in technologies such as HTML, DREAMWEAVER, Microsoft applications, etc. The logic behind this center is to create an information technology literate faculty that can then take on IT functions that might be assumed by IT departments in some other universities.

The Center is also responsible for teaching adaptive technologies, many of which are designed for the disabled, to enable them to take advantage of the broad range of facilities offered by the Library and the broader University. However, many of these courses are also taken by others since they cover a range of technologies – voice recognition or scanning, for example – which can be profitably used by all. The Center is physically housed in the Library; its director reports to the Chief Librarian, though its staff is trained in technology-oriented (often hands-on) type subjects and not in library science per se. The Center offered 152 classes in 2002; a total of 2,731 faculty and TA's attended the classes.

Although the Center's classes for instructors tend to be heavily attended, the Library's "drop-in" classes for students tend to be somewhat sparsely attended. "We are re-thinking the content of these," notes Mendelsohn. The Library has also recently embarked on an internal marketing campaign to alert faculty members to the "on request" classes given by Library staff in the context of for-credit courses in other disciplines.

REFERENCE TRAFFIC

As with many major research libraries, traditional in-library and telephone reference traffic has slowed, at least measured on a headcount basis. However, Mendelsohn notes that "it tends to take longer to help each inquirer since our resources are more complicated. It is not that we are less busy – people need a lot more help than they used to."

Newman adds that the Library is looking into virtual reference, and "We are exploring options but it has been very slow moving."

ONTARIO'S HIGH TECH INDUSTRY AND ITS IMPACT ON THE UNIVERSITY LIBRARY

In recent years the Canadian economy has gradually transformed itself from one based to a far greater extent than the US economy on agriculture, extractive industries and heavy manufacturing to one based more on services and high technology industries. Toronto, Montreal and Vancouver are now considered major high tech industry centers in the same class as Silicon Valley, Boston and Research Triangle Park.

As Ontario provincial and Canadian Federal officials more greatly emphasize high tech competitiveness, the University of Toronto has benefited from government largesse to develop its information technology resources. The changes that have affected and will continue to affect the Library's approach to information literacy.

The University has recently unveiled the new Bahan Center for Information Technology, a multidisciplinary center for exploring information technology resources. The strongly supportive environment for new information technologies has also directly helped the Library to develop a new tool that will be made available to students and faculty at all Ontario universities – an enormous database dubbed "The Scholars Portal". The portal will give all students and faculty in all Ontario universities full text access to 10,000 (ten thousand) full text journals, 99% of which are peer reviewed. Newman hopes that the comprehensiveness and ease of use of this broad based tool will encourage Ontario students to use a broader range of scholarly resources, and that they will benefit from information literacy training at the point of need. In other words, as the information becomes more accessible, and more seek it out, more will also seek out the basic but enormously affective basic training that will enable them to exploit the Scholar's Portal and other library resources.

In our view, the Scholar's Portal may have the same impact on scholarly research that Infotrac and other basic full text databases had on popular research. Its ease of use drew the uninitiated into research and spurred the growth of information literacy on the popular level.

INTEGRATION OF INFO LITERACY SKILLS INTO VARIOUS UNIVERSITY FACULTIES

In many ways various UT faculties are working towards an increasing integration of library/information science skills into their programs, sometimes in ways that lead to information literacy requirements. The University of Toronto at Mississauga (a suburban satellite campus of U Toronto) is currently creating a for-credit library skills course-taught by a librarian but directly under the auspices of the Faculty of Arts & Sciences.

U Toronto's School of Education --The Ontario Institute for Studies in Education – offers a non-credit course run by the Library. This course is now being offered at a distance to distance ed students at the Institute. Librarians and educators from the Institute co-teach the course, dubbed "The Virtual Library". The University of Toronto Law School is also considering the idea of integrating library skills instruction into its curriculum.

LIBRARY EDUCATION EFFORTS THROUGH STUDENT OUTREACH SERVICES

While the University of Toronto does not require nor offer a basic English composition course, it does make available extensive help to students on the writing process through a series of writing centers. Within the context of these centers, librarians offer drop in sessions on library research skill acquisition. The Library also works with a college division called Counseling and Learning Services, which offers a combination of classes, tutoring and counseling for students confronting the rigors of academic life. In addition to critical basic academic and research skills, Counseling and Learning Services offers sessions on how to deal with stress, time management and other issues that impact academic performance. The Library has had significant success reaching students through the service.

Mendelsohn notes: "We just put on a week long series of seminars called 'Library Research from Start to Finish', the first time we had ever run something like this. We did 5 one-hour sessions and about 150 students passed through and the feedback was phenomenal. We are going to do it again."

PRG feels that the concept of reaching out to students in difficulty, academic or otherwise, with brief but highly focused library skill training, is an idea that has broad application at many institutions of higher education, perhaps particularly those in the United States. Many undergraduates and, indeed, many graduate students, feel overwhelmed by their early research experiences. In our highly wired digital era, students may be more reluctant than in the past to admit to ignorance of digital resources. The digital divide is also an important phenomenon to consider. Students from poorer backgrounds come to college far less exposed and far less well prepared in computer and internet technologies than their more affluent peers; they may need some additional assistance to get up to speed, particularly at research oriented universities at which the majority of students will tend to come from affluent backgrounds and highly wired homes. Most research suggests that this divide is wider in the United States than in Canada.

ADVICE TO OTHER LIBRARIES

Mendelsohn and Newman's advice might be summarized as follows:

- When confronted with limited resources, reach out to the Teaching Assistants: "We need to focus on searching with the TA's as a way of reaching large numbers of undergraduates."

- Give assignments that call on students to use library resources to solve immediate course-related problems that potentially impact their grade. "We already have a very good model in the biology 150 class. They are given minimal information on an article and they need to go out and find and identify it. Then they carry through on the article and they have to work through the evaluation of that article. The most effective learning takes place when there is a clear and immediate need and in some areas we have been able to do that. Doing is better than passive listening

- "We have to push at every level of the university – make sure that they recognize the importance of information skills."

- "Keep working at ongoing relationship with the faculty for whom we teach; we have to connect; we must keep connecting with them."

Other Reports From Primary Research Group Inc

CREATING THE VIRTUAL REFERENCE SERVICE
Publication Date: January 2003   Price: $85.00   ISBN#: 1-57440-058-4

This study profiles the efforts of academic, legal and public libraries to develop virtual reference services. Includes profiles of The Library of Congress, Yale University Law School, the Denver Public Library, Cleveland Public Library, Pennsylvania State University, Baruch College, MIT and many other institutions.

LAW LIBRARY BENCHMARKS
 Publication Date: December 2002 Price: $110.00   ISBN#: 1-57440-057-6

This special report presents more than 400 tables of data from a survey of 80 law libraries, mostly libraries of major law firms, law schools and courthouses. The report presents data on web and internet use, use of Westlaw and Lexis, use of CD-ROM, print and electronic books, print and electronic journals, and many other information vehicles. Data is broken out by type and size of library for easier benchmarking.

THE SURVEY OF ACADEMIC LIBRARIES, 2002 Edition
Publication Date: June 2002   ISBN#: 1-57440-052-2

The Survey of Academic Libraries presents the results of a survey of 66 academic libraries, with data broken out by size and type of library for easier benchmarking. Covers DC-ROM, web use, electronic and print journals, electronic and print directories, on line services and much more.

THE SURVEY OF COLLEGE MARKETING PROGRAMS
Publication Date: 2002   Price: $244.50

This landmark study of college marketing practices imparts critical benchmarking data now broken out by Carnegie Class for even better benchmarking performance. Hundreds of tables of data and commentary describe how American colleges and universities market themselves to prospective students. 92 American colleges and universities participated, including: 11 major research universities 22 baccalaureate-level colleges, 21 masters-granting colleges, 4 - theology institutes, and 25 community or junior colleges. Covers traditional marketing, internet marketing, and much more.

SURVEY OF ADULT & CONTINUING EDUCATION PROGRAMS IN HIGHER EDUCATION
Price: $183.50   Publication Date: October 1999

The Survey of Adult & Continuing Education Programs in Higher Education presents the findings of a detailed survey of college adult and continuing education programs, focusing on their revenues and expenditures, advertising and marketing practices, technology use practices, course offerings, student demographics, and other aspects of continuing & adult education program management.

DIGITAL CONTENT MARKETS FOR PUBLISHERS OF BOOKS, MAGAZINES, RESEARCH REPORTS, NEWSPAPERS, JOURNALS, NEWSLETTERS, & DIRECTORIES
Price: $1695.00   Publication Date: January, 2002

This special report from Primary Research Group is based on more than 500 interviews with publishers, aggregators, and information end users. The report presents detailed data on the overall market for text-based digital content, and breaks out the market by segment for publishers of books, newsletters, trade magazines, consumer magazines, journals, research reports, newspapers, directories and mailing lists. The report also looks at certain institutional and subject areas such as publishing by colleges, publishing by trade associations, and medical and legal publishing. Data in the report is based on 300 interviews with North American publishing companies and distributors, as well as 200 interviews with end users in corporations and libraries. For each type of publication, and for selected areas of publishing defined by the subject matter or type of parent institution, the report presents data on: 1) current and planned use of digital storefronts and other types of web content distribution, 2) spending to build digital distribution infrastructure, 3) use of third party syndicators such as QPASS and Isyndicate, 4) distribution through major commercial online services, 5) use of html, Microsoft Word, pdf and Asci, 6) current or planned use of encryption technology, 7) % of total content sales through digital sales, 8) % of ad revenues through online sources, 9) % of new order for print products through web site, 10) assessment of impact of digital publishing on print revenues, 11) % of print content available on the web, 12) % of digital content available in print format, 13) plans to make available print content on the web, 14) availability of content in CD-ROM, 15) comparison of CD-ROM to web distribution revenues, 16) web site development costs, 17) web site hosting costs. 18) Frequency of editing the web site, 19) web site outsourcing policies and other factors in digital publishing.

US CORPORATE MARKETS FOR DISTANCE LEARNING & ONLINE TRAINING
Special Discount Price for Colleges & Universities:
Price: $1895 Special price for (accredited colleges only): $1195.00
Publication Date: March 2001

This special report, sold to industry for almost $2,000.00, presents the results of a survey of more than 400 U.S. companies. The report breaks out the use of distance learning by type of industry, company size and other variables useful to marketers of online training. The report is designed to help vendors to quickly ascertain levels of current and future demand for online training and distance learning courses. Survey data is supplemented by with secondary data from SEC filings, government and trade association sources and other secondary sources to provide a complete overview of corporate markets for distance learning in the USA.

CREATING THE DIGITAL LIBRARY
Publication Date: April 2000   Price: $75.00   isbn#: 1-57440-047-9

This report profiles the efforts of major American and Canadian corporate, academic, legal, medical, public and other libraries to digitize their collections and otherwise develop and distribute digital content. Compare your libraries efforts to those of some of North America's most prominent libraries. Includes coverage of copyright issues, technical issues, negotiations with publishers and electronic information services, and other issues relovent to the development of the digital library.
Written by Cheryl Knott Malone, Assistant Professor of Library Science at the Graduate School of Library & Information Science, the College of Illinois at Urbana., and James Moses, President of Primary Research Group.

COPYRIGHT INFORMATION PURCHASING AND USAGE: BEST PRACTICES OF AMERICAN CORPORATIONS
Publication Date: October 2001   Price: $295.00

Based on interviews with more than a dozen major American corporations and government agencies, and includ: detailed profiles of FORD MOTOR COMPANY, THE US DEPARTMENT OF STATE, COMP~ ., MICROSOFT, LUCENT TECHNOLOGIES, AAB, and other companies and agencies.

COMING SOON: Call for Details:
Creating the Digital Medical Library
Creating the Digital Law Library